The Gradual Gain

Strategies for Sustainable Financial Growth

Andrew Galowey

Copyright © [Andrew Galowey] [2024]. All rights reserved. No part of this publication may be reproduced, distributed, or transmitted in any form or by any means, including photocopying, recording, or other electronic or mechanical methods, without the prior written permission of the publisher, except in the case of brief quotations embodied in critical reviews and certain other noncommercial uses permitted by copyright law.

Table Of Contents

Introduction

Chapter 1: Building Your Foundation: Budgeting for Growth

Chapter 2: Developing Responsible Investing Habits

Chapter 3: Taming the Debt Dragon

Chapter 4: Making Your Money Work for You

Chapter 5: Maximizing Retirement Savings

Chapter 6: The Gradual Gain Mindset: Developing Long-Term Financial Success

Introduction

ever desired financial freedom? Of witnessing your money develop consistently and achieving your long-term objectives without stress? While the world typically glorifies get-rich-quick schemes, genuine financial stability stems from a more practical approach: incremental prosperity.

This book, "The Gradual Gain: Strategies for Sustainable Financial Growth," provides a road map for attaining precisely that. Forget about dangerous fads and misleading promises. Here, we'll concentrate on laying a strong foundation, forming good financial habits, and applying techniques that assure continuous and long-term development. Whether you're just getting started with your finances or want to improve your current plan, this book provides essential insights and specific actions to help you walk the road to financial well-being.

So strap up and prepare to go on a voyage of steady gains. We'll look at budgeting for development, developing appropriate investment habits, and discovering how to make your money work for you. We will discuss debt management, income production techniques, and how to optimize your retirement funds. Most importantly, we'll assist you in developing the "gradual gain mindset" - a strong method that stresses consistency and long-term planning above passing trends.

Are you prepared to take charge of your financial future? Let us begin!

Chapter 1: Building Your Foundation: Budgeting for Growth

Any effective construction is built on a solid foundation. The same concept applies to your financial well-being. Budgeting is essential for long-term financial progress because it gives you a clear view of your income and spending, allowing you to make smart financial choices.

This chapter will show you how to create a rock-solid budget that promotes development. We'll look at the fundamentals of budgeting, identify useful tools and tactics, and provide you the information you need to construct a specific strategy for attaining your financial objectives.

Why budget?
Many people associate budgeting with a negative connotation: a rigid system that takes the joy out of spending. The reality is just the reverse. Budgeting empowers you. It gives you a feeling of control over your

money by enabling you to monitor your progress, detect spending trends, and strategically allocate resources toward your objectives.

Here are some major advantages of budgeting:

- Gaining Control: A well-defined budget helps you understand your financial status. You'll know precisely where your money goes, enabling you to pinpoint areas where you can cut down and free up funds for savings and investments.
- Prioritizing Goals: A budget may help you identify your financial objectives. Do you want a pleasant retirement? A debt-free future? A fantasy vacation? A budget guarantees that you are allocating finances effectively towards your objectives.
- Making Informed choices: Knowing your income and spending will allow

you to confidently make informed financial choices. A budget gives a strong foundation for analysis, whether you're contemplating a large purchase or deciding on an investing plan.
- Reducing Financial Stress: Financial uncertainty is a major cause of stress. Budgeting removes the uncertainty and gives piece of mind by ensuring that your spending is in line with your income and long-term objectives.

Building Your Budget

Are you ready to take charge of your finances? Here's how to make a budget that works for you.

- Gather Your Information: The first step is to compile all of your financial data. This includes your pay stubs, bank statements, credit card bills, and any other regular costs.

- Track Your revenue: Make a list of all your revenue sources, such as salaries, bonuses, side hustles, and rental money. To obtain a comprehensive picture, include as much information as possible.
- Categorize Your Expenses: This is where most people go stuck. Don't worry, start small. Begin by organizing your spending into broad categories like as housing, utilities, food, transportation, and entertainment. Later, you may refine them (for example, grocery vs. eating out).
- Track Your spending: For one month, precisely record all of your spending. Use a budgeting tool, a spreadsheet, or pen and paper, whatever works best for you. This gives critical data for gaining a true insight of your purchasing patterns.
- Analyze Your Findings: Here comes the magic. Compare your income and spending. Are there any places where

you might cut back? Are there any hidden costs you hadn't considered?
- Set Realistic Financial objectives: Determine your income and spending before setting financial objectives. Aim to save a set amount each month, pay off debt, or contribute a certain percentage to retirement.
- Create Your Budget: Now it's time to put together your real budget. Allocate cash according to your income and desired savings objectives. Be realistic but hopeful. Remember that your budget should be an adaptable tool, not a fixed limitation.

Budget Tools and Strategies
There are many budgeting tools and solutions available. Here are a few common choices:

The 50/30/20 Rule states that you should spend 50% of your income on necessities (housing, electricity, and food), 30% on desires (entertainment and eating out), and 20% on savings and debt reduction. It's an excellent starting place, but adjust it to your individual requirements.

- Zero-Based Budgeting: This strategy allocates every dollar of your revenue to a specified purpose, guaranteeing that no money is left unallocated at the end of the month. It demands dedication but provides an accurate view of your financial status.
- Budgeting applications: Several budgeting applications make the process easier. These applications let you monitor income and expenditures, classify spending, and create savings goals all from your smartphone.

Make Your Budget Work for You

A successful budget is a dynamic document, not a static one. Here's how to make sure your budget continues to help you when your financial condition changes:

Review your budget on a regular basis to verify that it accurately represents your actual income and spending trends.
- Be adaptable: Life throws curveballs. Unexpected expenditures may occur. Adjust your budget appropriately while remaining committed to your ultimate objectives.
- Celebrate Your Achievements: Reaching milestones, no matter how minor, reinforces positive

Chapter 2: Developing Responsible Investing Habits

Congratulations! You've established a strong budget as the cornerstone for your financial progress. Now it's time to go into the realm of investing, where your money may actually begin to work for you. But, before we dive in, let's build ethical financial habits that will assure long-term success.

This chapter will provide you with the information and skills you need to become a more attentive investor. We'll look at several investing possibilities, assess your risk tolerance, and help you design a diversified portfolio that corresponds with your objectives and beliefs.

Why invest?
Investing entails putting your money into assets with the intention of future growth. It's an effective method for accumulating money over time, enabling you to

outperform inflation and meet your financial goals.

Here are some fundamental reasons why responsible investment is important:

- Grow Your Wealth: While saving is crucial, investing has the potential to provide higher returns than standard savings accounts. Over time, your assets may increase significantly, assisting you in meeting long-term financial objectives such as retirement or a child's education.
- Reaching Your Goals: Investing enables you to achieve your financial objectives quicker. Whether it's a dream trip, a down payment on a home, or early retirement, investing may help close the gap between your present funds and your goals.
- Financial independence: Building money via ethical investing promotes financial independence. As your

assets grow, you gain control of your financial destiny, giving you more peace of mind and the freedom to follow your hobbies.

Understanding Your Risk Tolerance

Investing naturally carries risk. Some investments have the potential for significant profits but carry a greater level of risk. In contrast, some provide lesser risk but lower profits. Understanding your risk tolerance is critical before entering the financial environment.

Here are some elements to consider when evaluating your risk tolerance.

- Investment Time Horizon: When will you need the money? Long-term objectives (retirement) allow for a greater risk tolerance since time reduces short-term market volatility. Short-term objectives need more cautious investments.

- Financial objectives: What are you investing for? Some ambitions, like as a down payment on a home, may need more stability than a retirement account. Consider your risk tolerance for each individual aim.
- Financial Situation: Can you afford to lose money? A solid emergency fund serves as a safety net, enabling you to invest with a somewhat larger risk tolerance.

Building a Diversified Portfolio

Once you've determined your risk tolerance, it's time to create your investing portfolio. Diversification is the foundation of sensible investment. This entails spreading your assets across several asset types to reduce risk.

Here are some typical asset classes:

- Stocks represent company ownership. Stocks have the potential for large gains, but they also involve more risk.
- Bonds are loans issued to governments or enterprises. Bonds are good for conservative investors because they provide reduced risk and more consistent returns.
- Mutual funds are investment pools managed by experts that invest in a wide range of assets. Mutual funds provide diversity and expert management at a reasonable cost.
- Exchange-Traded Funds (ETFs): Similar to mutual funds, but traded on stock markets all day. ETFs provide diversity and cheap costs.
- Real estate investing, whether in physical property or real estate investment trusts (REITs), has the potential for long-term gain as well as rental income.

By intelligently distributing your assets across asset classes, you reduce risk and ensure that your portfolio is balanced and in line with your risk tolerance and financial objectives.

Responsible Investing: Beyond Asset Allocation

Responsible investment extends beyond merely selecting the appropriate asset types. Here are some more considerations for the prudent investor:

Socially Responsible Investing (SRI) is a technique that evaluates a company's environmental, social, and governance (ESG) concerns before investing. SRI enables you to connect your investments with your principles and support firms that have a good effect.

- costs and Expenses: Be aware of the costs connected with investments such as mutual funds and ETFs.

Lower costs might have a big influence on your long-term results.
- Long-term Perspective: Investing is a marathon, not a sprint. Avoid getting caught up in short-term market volatility. Maintain a long-term perspective and avoid making hasty judgments due to market volatility.

You may create responsible investing habits by diversifying your portfolio, evaluating socially responsible actions, and keeping a long-term perspective.

Chapter 3: Taming the Debt Dragon

Debt, although a frequent financial barrier, may greatly hamper your progress toward financial well-being. This chapter provides you with tactics for efficiently managing debt, creating a clear payback plan, and finally defeating the debt dragon.

We'll look at various sorts of debt, how they affect you, and walk you through the process of developing a specific plan to get out of debt.

Understanding Debt

Debt is simply borrowed money that must be returned with interest. Not all debt is created equally. Understanding the various forms of debt and their effects on your finances is critical for successful management.

Here's a summary of some typical debt categories:

1. Good Debt: This is debt utilized for investments with the potential to create returns greater than the interest rate. Mortgages, for example, are used to finance the purchase of a property, while student loans are used to invest in your future earnings potential.
2. Bad debt often has high interest rates and provides no genuine long-term value. Credit card debt, payday loans, and title loans are among examples. These sorts of debt may soon get out of hand, impeding your financial success.

While good debt may be a strategic instrument for wealth accumulation, bad debt must be addressed straight on. Here are some essential tactics for managing, and eventually eradicating, bad debt:

Developing a Debt Repayment Plan

The first step toward debt freedom is developing a clear and effective repayment plan. Here is how to start:

Make a complete inventory of all your debts, including their outstanding balances, interest rates, and minimum monthly payments.
- Prioritize Your Debts: Not all debts are the same. Prioritize high-interest obligations first since the interest compounded fast, increasing the overall cost over time. There are two commonly used prioritizing strategies:
- The Avalanche Method: Pay off the loan with the highest interest rate first, regardless of amount. This saves you the most money on interest rates overall.
- The Snowball Method: Pay off the debt with the lowest amount first, regardless of interest rate. Seeing debts go rapidly might motivate you and keep you on track.

- Calculate Your Additional Payments: Once you've prioritized your bills, figure out how much more money you can put towards debt repayment each month. This might include reducing unneeded spending or finding strategies to boost your income.

Strategies for Debt Repayment

You're ready to take on your debt now that you have a clear strategy in place. Here are some efficient ways to speed your payback journey:

- The Debt Snowball/Avalanche Method in Action: Use your preferred prioritizing approach (avalanche or snowball) and direct your increased payments to the targeted debt while making minimum payments on the rest.
- Debt Consolidation: Consider combining numerous high-interest loans into a single loan with a reduced

interest rate. This streamlines the repayment procedure and might help you save money on interest.
- Negotiate Lower Interest Rates: Contact your creditors and try to negotiate lower interest rates, particularly if you have a history of timely payments.
- Increase Your Income: Look at methods to supplement your income via side hustles, freelance employment, or negotiating a raise. This higher revenue enables you to put more money towards debt reduction.

Living Debt-free

Congratulations for conquering the debt dragon! But the trip does not stop there. Here are some strategies for living a debt-free lifestyle:

- Maintain a Budget: A well-defined budget allows you to keep track of

your expenditures and avoid accumulating unneeded debt.
- Pay Your Bills on Time: Making it a practice to pay your bills on time helps you keep a solid credit score, which may be useful in the future when applying for loans or credit cards.
- Use Credit Cards Responsibly: If you decide to use credit cards, pay them off in full each month to prevent accruing interest charges.
- Save for Emergencies: Create an emergency fund to meet unforeseen expenditures and prevent going into debt in times of need.

Implementing these tactics will allow you to efficiently manage debt, develop a clear payback plan, and eventually attain a debt-free future, paving the way for a more secure and profitable financial journey.

Chapter 4: Making Your Money Work for You

Wouldn't it be great if your money helped you achieve your financial objectives even while you slept? This chapter delves into ideas for putting your money to work for you and earning money in addition to your normal wage.

We'll look at revenue production strategies such as side hustles, passive income sources, and utilizing your abilities for extra money. By applying these tactics, you may improve your money and open up new opportunities.

Beyond the Paycheck: Exploring Income Generation

Traditionally, our revenue comes from a single source: our paycheck. However, the financial environment provides several opportunities to produce extra money, enabling you to accelerate your financial growth and reach your objectives more quickly.

Here are some significant advantages of investigating revenue production opportunities outside your paycheck:

- Increased Financial Security: Having many revenue sources offers a financial safety net. If your major source of income is interrupted, having extra money might help you stay afloat and weather financial storms.
- Earning more money helps you to save and invest more aggressively, which accelerates your progress toward financial milestones such as early retirement or a dream trip.
- Greater Financial Freedom: Having many revenue sources allows you to be less dependent on a single source. This promotes financial freedom and

allows you to follow your hobbies and professional goals.

The Side Hustle Revolution
The side hustle revolution has changed the way individuals make money. Side hustles are part-time activities that you undertake in addition to your main work. They often capitalize on your current talents or interests while providing flexibility in terms of time commitment and earning possibilities.

Here are some common side hustles to consider:

- Freelancing: Share your talents and knowledge on freelancing sites such as Upwork or Fiverr. This might include writing, editing, graphic design, programming, or virtual help jobs.
- The Sharing Economy: Platforms like Airbnb and Turo enable you to rent out underused assets such as your spare

room or vehicle, earning money while you're not using them.
- Sell Your Crafts or Handmade Goods: Do you have a talent for creating jewelry, ceramics, and other crafts? Sell your items online on platforms such as Etsy or at local craft fairs.
- Provide Online Services: Depending on your area of expertise, you may provide online tuition, consultancy, or language classes.
- Blogging or vlogging allows you to share your expertise and enthusiasm. While it takes time to grow an audience, effective content producers may make money via advertising, affiliate marketing, or selling their own goods or services.

The secret to a successful side hustle is to pick an activity you like or are skilled at, and then package it into a worthwhile service or product for others.

The allure of passive income

Passive income is money obtained with minimum continuous effort. While it may need some initial effort to establish, the benefit of passive income is that it continues to trickle in over time.

Here are several methods to get passive income:

- Rental Properties: Investing in rental properties offers a consistent source of income via rent payments. However, it needs active management or the engagement of a property management firm.
- Peer-to-peer lending: Platforms such as LendingClub link you with borrowers looking for loans. By investing in these loans, you may earn interest on your repayments.
- Dividend-Paying companies: Investing in dividend-paying companies might help you produce passive income.

However, the stock market has inherent hazards.
- Royalties: If you are a creative person, such as a musician, novelist, or photographer, your work may produce royalties when it is used or sold.

While passive income sources may demand an initial commitment or work, the long-term advantages of recurring income are very appealing.

Leveraging Your Skills

Consider your present skill set and how you may use it to produce more revenue. Here are a few ideas:

- Teach a Skill: Do you have a special gift or expertise? Offer online classes or seminars to share your expertise.
- Write an E-book: If you have writing talents and understanding in a certain field, try creating and self-publishing an e-book.

- design an App or Online Course: If you have a technical background or experience in a certain field, you may design and sell an app or online course.

By recognizing your abilities and researching new methods to commercialize them, you may open up a plethora of income-generating opportunities.

Remember that making money work for you is a marathon, not a sprint. Be patient, try multiple tactics, and concentrate on creating long-term revenue streams that suit your financial objectives and lifestyle.

Chapter 5: Maximizing Retirement Savings

Planning for a safe and enjoyable retirement is an important part of obtaining financial stability. This chapter digs into the world of retirement savings vehicles, guiding you through your choices and maximizing your contributions to secure a golden age free of financial worries.

We'll look at popular retirement accounts including IRAs and 401(k)s, discuss contribution limitations and tax breaks, and provide you with methods for making the most of your retirement savings efforts.

Why should I plan for retirement?
While retirement may seem distant, particularly for younger people, the power of compound interest necessitates early preparation. Compound interest permits your donations to increase exponentially over time, considerably boosting your retirement savings.

Here are a few important reasons to prioritize retirement savings:

- Financial stability: A well-funded retirement plan ensures financial stability in your senior years. You won't have to rely only on Social Security, enabling you to live the lifestyle you choose without financial concern.
- Peace of Mind: Knowing that you have a secure future helps you to fully enjoy your retirement years without worrying about money.
- Maintaining Independence: Proper retirement preparation allows you to remain independent and avoid depending on others for financial help in retirement.

Retirement Savings Vehicles

There are various retirement savings vehicles available, each with its own set of advantages and disadvantages. Understanding these possibilities is critical for making sound judgments and maximizing your contributions. Here are a few common options:

- A classic IRA (Individual Retirement Account) enables you to deduct your contributions from your current taxable income, thereby lowering your tax liability. Earnings from your contributions grow tax-free until you withdraw them in retirement, when they are taxed as income. Traditional IRAs have yearly contribution restrictions.

- Roth IRA: Contributions to a Roth IRA are made after tax, but any qualifying withdrawals (including both contributions and profits) are tax-free after retirement. Roth IRAs provide more flexibility in terms of accessing funds prior to retirement, but eligibility is subject to income limits.

- 401(k): Many workplaces offer 401(k) plans, which enable you to contribute a percentage of your income before taxes are taken. This lowers your taxable income while allowing your contributions to grow tax-deferred. Some businesses provide matching contributions, which are basically free money that increases your retirement savings. There are yearly contribution restrictions for 401(k) accounts.

Some non-profit organizations and public schools provide 403(b) plans, which are similar to 401(k)s. Contributions are paid before taxes and accumulate tax-deferred until withdrawn at retirement.

Choosing the Right Retirement Account
The appropriate retirement account for you is determined by your financial condition

and long-term aspirations. Here are some things to consider:

- Tax Bracket: Traditional IRAs provide upfront tax deductions, which help those in higher tax rates. Roth IRAs allow you tax-free withdrawals in retirement, which might be beneficial depending on your predicted tax level.

If you intend to retire early, a Roth IRA may be a better alternative since you may receive your contributions without penalty before reaching age 59 ½.

- business Matching: If your business matches contributions to a 401(k), maximize those contributions since they are practically free money for your retirement.

Maximize Your Retirement Savings

Beyond merely selecting the appropriate account, here are several techniques to optimize your retirement savings:

- Begin Early: The power of compound interest is considerable. Starting to save early enables your contributions to rise tremendously over time.
- boost Contributions on a Regular Basis: Aim to boost your retirement contributions at least once a year, even if it is a modest amount. As your salary increases, put a bigger share to retirement savings.
- Take Advantage of workplace Matching: If your workplace provides matching contributions, be sure to maximize them in order to get the most out of this free money.
- Automate Your Savings: Establish automatic payments to your retirement account. This guarantees that you save regularly and removes the temptation to spend the money elsewhere.
- Utilize Catch-Up Contributions: The IRS permits persons 50 and older to make extra "catch-up" contributions to

their retirement accounts each year. This enables them to save more aggressively and maybe compensate for previous years' lower contributions.

By adopting a proactive attitude, using accessible retirement savings vehicles, and applying these tactics, you may assure a safe and pleasant financial future in retirement.

Chapter 6: The Gradual Gain Mindset: Developing Long-Term Financial Success

Financial well-being does not happen overnight. It's a journey fuelled by hard work, educated judgments, and a development attitude. This chapter discusses the need of developing a progressive gain attitude for long-term financial success.

We'll look at the psychology of money, how to remain motivated, and how to adjust your financial strategy when your objectives and circumstances change.

Beyond Strategy: The Power of Mindset
The techniques presented in this book are useful tools for managing your financial path. But genuine financial success is dependent on your thinking. Developing a progressive gain attitude lays the groundwork for long-term financial stability.

Here's what a gradual gain attitude involves:

- Focus on Progress, Not Perfection: Acknowledge that financial progress is a long process. Celebrate minor victories; failures are unavoidable; learn from them, and keep going ahead.
- Long-Term Perspective: Financial objectives such as retirement or financial independence may seem distant. Maintain a long-term perspective, stick to your strategy, and believe in the power of compound interest.
- Patience is essential: accumulating money requires time and discipline. Avoid get-rich-quick scams and instead concentrate on steady, long-term methods.
- Embrace Change: Your financial requirements and aspirations will change over time. Be adaptive and

open to change your methods as needed.
- Lifelong Learning: The financial environment is continuously changing. Stay educated, continue to learn about personal finance, and adjust your strategy depending on fresh information.

By adopting a progressive gain attitude, you'll be better prepared to deal with the inevitable ups and downs of your financial path.

Understanding The Psychology of Money
Our financial habits are often impacted by our thoughts and feelings toward money. Understanding these underlying psychological issues is critical to establishing a successful financial relationship.

Consider the following fundamental features of the psychology of money:

- Money Scripts: These are unconscious views about money that we form throughout our lives, frequently influenced by our family and cultural background. Identifying your money scripts can help you better understand your spending patterns and financial choices.
- Emotional Spending: Do you spend impulsively to deal with stress or emotions? Recognizing this habit is the first step toward controlling emotional spending and making sound financial choices.
- Fear of FOMO (Fear of Missing Out): Social media and advertising bombard us with pictures of opulent lifestyles. Avoid comparing yourself to others and making financial choices based on FOMO. Align your expenditures with your own objectives and ideals.

Understanding the psychology of money may help you break free from bad financial habits and build a more thoughtful attitude to money.

Staying Motivated in Your Financial Journey
Maintaining motivation is critical for long-term financial success. Here are some ways to help you stay on track:

Set SMART objectives that are specific, measurable, achievable, relevant, and time-bound. This creates a clear road map for your financial path, allowing you to measure progress and celebrate accomplishments.
- Visualize Your Goals: Imagine yourself reaching your financial objectives. Create a vision board or write down your objectives in detail. This might help you maintain motivation and attention during difficult circumstances.

- Find a Financial Accountability Partner: Discuss your financial objectives with a trustworthy friend or family member who can provide support and encouragement.
- Reward Yourself: Celebrate your achievements along the way. This encourages excellent financial practices and motivates you to continue your quest.
- Stay Positive: Concentrate on your development and enjoy tiny victories. Don't be disheartened by failures; instead, consider them as learning opportunities.

By applying these tactics, you may build a positive and motivated mentality that will propel your financial path.

Adapting Strategies for Long-term Success

Life throws curveballs. Your financial requirements and ambitions will undoubtedly change over time. Here's how to keep your financial plans relevant:

- Regularly Review Your Budget and objectives: As circumstances change, it is important to examine your budget and financial objectives on a regular basis. Adjust your plans as required to ensure they meet your present demands and future goals.
- Embrace New Knowledge: The financial landscape changes. Stay updated about new financial tools and techniques that may help you improve your financial situation.
- Be adaptable: life is unexpected. Be prepared to change your strategy if you encounter unanticipated financial obstacles or possibilities.

Developing a progressive gain attitude enables you to adapt and welcome change. This guarantees you have the necessary skills and mentality to manage the ever-changing world of personal finance and achieve long-term financial success.

Remember that generating money is a marathon, not a sprint. Embrace the process, adopt a steady gain attitude, and enjoy the financial independence that awaits you!

www.ingramcontent.com/pod-product-compliance
Lightning Source LLC
Chambersburg PA
CBHW050247230526
45470CB00005B/2149